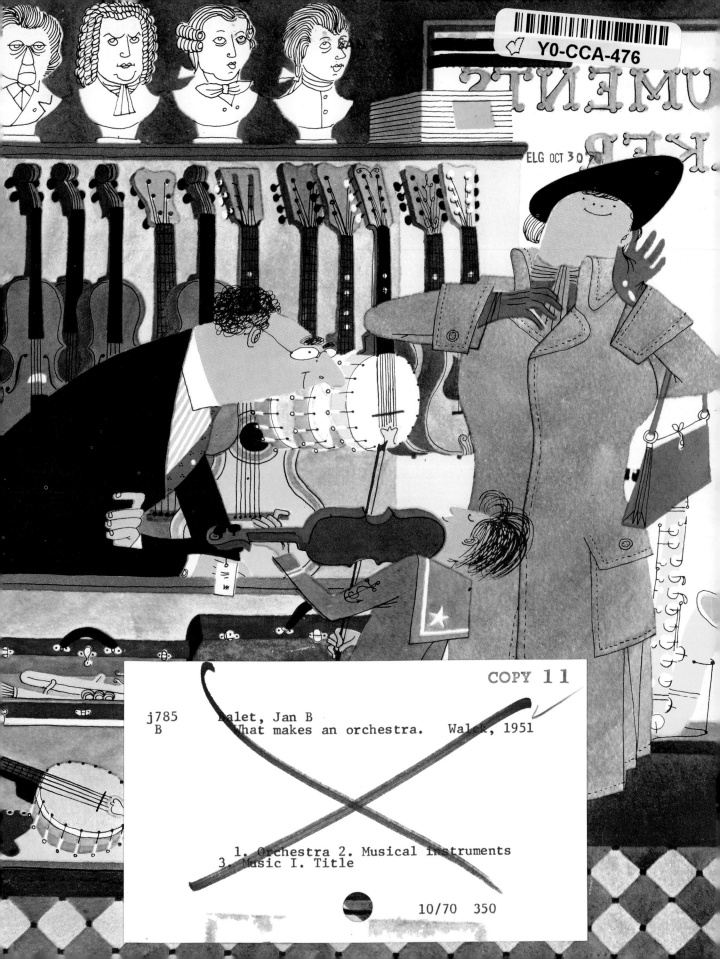

WHAT MAKES

HENRY Z. WALCK, INCORPORATED

STORY AND PICTURES BY
JAN BALET

AN ORCHESTRA

For Lisa

COPYRIGHT 1951 HENRY Z. WALCK, INC.

LIBRARY OF CONGRESS CATALOG CARD NUMBER: 59-15225

● The violin is often called the king of the orchestra because most of the time, when you hear an orchestra, you hear the wonderful rich singing tones of violins. In fact, when the violins and their sisters (the violas, 'cellos and double basses) are all silent, we no longer have an orchestra — we have a brass band. Put one end of a rubber band between your teeth and stretch it with your left hand. Now pluck it lightly with the fingers of your right hand. Can you feel your teeth tingle? Can you hear a musical tone? You will hear the tone change if you stretch the band or shorten it or if you use bands of different thicknesses. Music on the violin is produced in much the same way. Usually, however, the strings are not plucked; instead

a bow is passed over them to make them vibrate. Violins in an orchestra can do many things. They can play fairly low or very high. They can whisper so that you have to "stretch" your ears, or they can make your eyes almost pop with their shrillness. They can lull you to sleep or startle you like a flash of lightning. They can make you feel sad, or warm and good all over. They can play slowly, oh, so very slowly, or so fast that your heart jumps as if you were in a rushing roller coaster. Indeed, no instrument can do all the violin can do. Listen for the effects of the player's fingers when they pluck the strings, when the fingers of the left hand flutter back and forth like restless birds, or when the bows bounce on the strings. How marvelous it is that this instrument which looks like an empty wooden box with four strings across it should be able to produce such magical sounds! The truth is that it is much more than a simple box. Many men worked for generations to fit together its more than seventy separate parts until they gave us the perfect instrument of today — an instrument which "plays second fiddle" to none.

3

● The viola is played like the violin and looks so much like it that at first you do not see that it is a little larger. But when you hear it, what a difference! Its voice is older and deeper. You feel as when you first heard a midget speak. He may have looked no bigger than a little boy but he spoke with the voice of a grown man. The viola sounds low and dark because it is tuned lower than the violin. Its tone is not as round or brilliant as the violin's, but it is stronger. That is why a dozen violas can hold their own with as many as thirty-two first and second violins. In the orchestra the violas take the lead now and then, but most of the time they play in combination with other instruments. The viola can tell a story that is sad or full of pain. When it sounds sharp or nasal, you feel restless. If the mysterious Sphinx could speak, it would have the shadowy voice of a viola.

● Each member of the string family, like the three bears, is bigger than the last. The cello is so big that it cannot be held in the player's hands but has to rest on the floor between his knees. Its sound, too, is big, strong, deep and very rich. Even its name, violoncello, is big. We call it cello for short. Everyone loves the cello — not only the people who listen to music but the men who write it. Its mellow, almost human baritone voice often leads the whole orchestra. It thrills you and makes you want to sing along. It can sing of love and hope and high ambition. It can sing of beauty and goodness and of sadness, too. Can you remember a time when your teacher held you spellbound with a story? That is how the cello's voice wins you to listen.

● People who play instruments, especially stringed instruments, are very friendly and like nothing better than to meet in one another's homes and play together. The music played by such groups is called "chamber music." After years of experimenting, it was found that the best sounding combination was the String Quartet which is a group of four stringed instruments — two violins (called first violin and second violin), a cello and a viola. At first, the four members of the String Quartet played together for their own amusement. But their music was so attractive and beautifully blended that many guests came just to listen. Today chamber music is quite popular and is often heard in large concert halls.

● The double bass is the largest instrument of the string family. It is taller than many of the men who play it. A tall player may stand behind it, but a short one has to sit on a high stool. It has tones that are so low that they do not sing. In the orchestra the double basses are rarely asked to take the lead or play fast. They are dry and rough and booming, or they seem to growl. Yet it is very important to have double basses in the orchestra. They act like ballast in the bottom of a ship. You do not see the ballast, but you know it is there or the ship would not be steady. In the same way, you often do not hear the double basses because they are far in the background. But if they should suddenly stop playing, you would feel that something is missing.

Pedal Action

● Look at the orchestra. The golden harp stands out clear. Its curves are as graceful as the player's arms and fingers as he plucks the strings of the harp much as you might play a guitar. It looks like the inside of a grand piano standing on end. The harp is not a busy instrument. It is used only at times when the music is meant to sound delicate, gentle and dainty. Its tones float in the air like a rainbow one can never forget. It reminds one of soft spring rain, of flowers bending in the breeze or of the light of the moon as it appears and disappears behind a veil of clouds. This instrument has been heard in many lands for thousands of years. The Irish loved the harp so much that they put it in their flag.

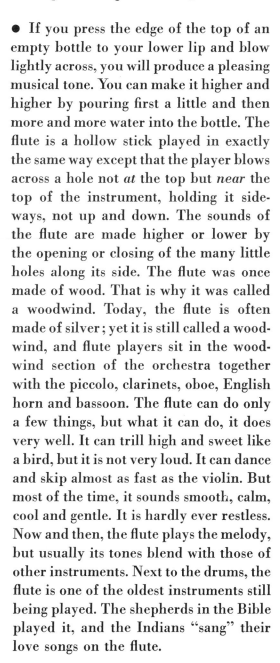

● If you press the edge of the top of an empty bottle to your lower lip and blow lightly across, you will produce a pleasing musical tone. You can make it higher and higher by pouring first a little and then more and more water into the bottle. The flute is a hollow stick played in exactly the same way except that the player blows across a hole not *at* the top but *near* the top of the instrument, holding it sideways, not up and down. The sounds of the flute are made higher or lower by the opening or closing of the many little holes along its side. The flute was once made of wood. That is why it was called a woodwind. Today, the flute is often made of silver; yet it is still called a woodwind, and flute players sit in the woodwind section of the orchestra together with the piccolo, clarinets, oboe, English horn and bassoon. The flute can do only a few things, but what it can do, it does very well. It can trill high and sweet like a bird, but it is not very loud. It can dance and skip almost as fast as the violin. But most of the time, it sounds smooth, calm, cool and gentle. It is hardly ever restless. Now and then, the flute plays the melody, but usually its tones blend with those of other instruments. Next to the drums, the flute is one of the oldest instruments still being played. The shepherds in the Bible played it, and the Indians "sang" their love songs on the flute.

10

● Just as a teacher's whistle can cut through all the clatter of a school yard full of children shouting at play, so the piercing voice of a single piccolo can be heard above all the instruments of the orchestra even when they are playing their loudest. It is a shrill and noisy imp with the highest voice in the orchestra. It can shriek; it can squeak, and be very bright and playful. It looks like a flute and it is played like one. Actually it is a "flauto piccolo"—a tiny or pocket-size flute. There is usually only one piccolo needed for a whole orchestra.

● The metronome is not a musical instrument. It goes tick-tick—beating time, fast or slow, according to the speed at which it is set. A player often uses it when he practises at home and has no conductor to beat time for him.

Double Reed

● Just as the cello is the favorite stringed instrument of many composers, so the oboe is the favorite woodwind. It is an old instrument, so old that it was known to the Egyptians six thousand years ago. The player's fingers move on it as they do on the flute, but the instrument is held up and down, and the player blows through two reeds held in his mouth. The oboe has a bitter-sweet, soft and very nasal voice. Its long drawn-out tones sound tender and sad although sometimes it can chuckle in fun. When the oboe sings alone, it seems to say, "Listen-to-me," and you wish it would play on and on. This the oboe cannot do. It has a problem all its own. The player must blow so gently that he can never let the air completely out of his lungs and he gets red-faced holding it back. This is such a strain that he must be allowed to rest longer and more often than players on other blowing instruments.

12

● The English horn has a long curved mouthpiece and a bell-shaped bottom. Although it is played like an oboe, its voice is different. It is lower, smoother, richer, more mellow and mysterious. It is also less nasal. If the oboe and the flute may be called the violins of the woodwinds, the English horn is the viola. Composers save this instrument for moments when they want you to daydream or feel lonely. Once you hear it, its lovely voice will return to haunt you for days to come. You may wonder why this woodwind instrument is called a "horn" and what makes it especially English. Nobody really knows for sure. Some people say that long ago all instruments using "wind" were called horns. This particular instrument was a "horn" with a curved mouthpiece—in other words, an "angled" mouthpiece. The French word for "angled" (*anglé*) sounds like the French word for "English" (*anglais*). So the story goes that people confused the two words.

● The members of a string quartet often invite a guest to add his talents to theirs. When such a group of five plays together, it is called a quintet.

● A listener once remarked that the oboe sounds as if it had a cold in its head; the bassoon, a cold in its chest. The comparison is good because the oboe has high nasal tones while the bassoon often produces low hoarse sounds. Think of it as a stretched-out oboe, six feet long. To make it less clumsy, it is cut into two sections, which are joined at the bottom in a narrow V. You may be sure you will hear low notes coming from the bassoon because the longer the tube through which the player blows, the lower the sound that comes forth. And the bassoon, as we saw, has a very long tube. Like many over-sized and clumsy people, the bassoon is jolly and loves company. So you often hear his hard dry voice chatting with the strings, other woodwinds, or the brasses. Sometimes they let him hold the stage alone, and then he growls comically in his bass wheezing voice. When he gets excited, he talks rapidly, but he still makes you laugh as if he were an elephant trying to dance.

Single Reed

● When a woodwind sounds especially smooth, rich and creamy, it is probably the clarinet. Its tone is less nasal than the oboe's and more reedy than the flute's. Its high notes are exciting when played fast. But it is more usual to hear it move slowly in a melody using tones which are not too high; then it sounds sweet and lovely. When it plays a melody using the low tones it sounds dark and sad and velvety. The clarinet looks like the oboe and is played in much the same way, but it has a single reed (see picture). It can produce many of the oboe's sound effects. Because it is easier to play, you are likely to hear it more often. The bassoon may be called the clown of the orchestra, but the clarinet which flies through the air so easily is the man on the flying trapeze. The bassoon makes you laugh, but the clarinet makes you smile or fills you with a sadness that is not sorrowful but like the sadness one feels when summer is fading away.

● The bàss clarinet is shaped like a saxophone. It is really a clarinet with a specially long tube having the lower end curved up and the neck curved down in order to make it easier to handle. Because its tube is longer than the clarinet's, its tone is deeper, more serious and more luscious. It cannot be played as fast. Its voice can sound mysterious and important, or windy and hollow. It is never gay or light-hearted. All of the woodwinds may be divided into three small groups. First, there are the instruments that have no reeds — flute and piccolo. Then come the instruments with a single reed in the mouthpiece — clarinet, and bass clarinet and saxophone. Last are oboe, English horn and bassoon, which have double reeds. But whether they have one reed or two or none at all, the woodwinds supply the more delicate tone-colors to the picture the whole orchestra is painting. Their voices are the pale blues, greens and pearly greys. The trumpets and trombones fill in the bold reds, bright blues and deep purples.

● The saxophone is frequently heard in popular dance bands. It is still not considered a regular member of the orchestra and is invited only for special occasions. It is named after Adolphe Sax who invented it a little more than a hundred years ago. It is really a large clarinet made of brass. This makes it sound half like the woodwinds and half like the horns. It is loud and shrill and brassy. It can sound very sorry for itself or very sarcastic, but the thing you remember about it most is its peculiar whining voice. Many composers feel that the saxophone is not needed in the orchestra. According to them, what it can do best, other instruments already in the orchestra can do as well. Because it sounds better in the open and the performer can easily carry and play it while walking, the saxophone is more at home in a brass band. Like most other instruments, it comes in different sizes. Going from the smallest to the largest we have the soprano, the alto, the tenor, the baritone, the bass and other saxophones, twelve in all. The smallest with the shortest tube has the highest voice and the largest with the longest tube sings the lowest.

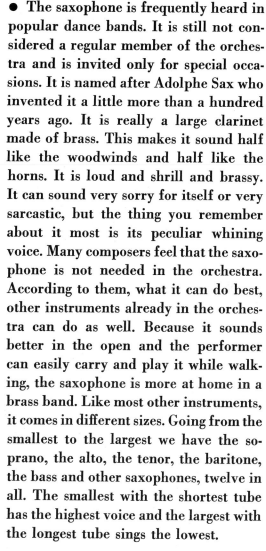

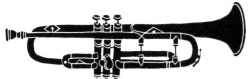

● The trumpet is a shiny golden instrument with a dazzling far-carrying voice. Like all brass instruments, it has a long coiled tube with a mouthpiece against which the player presses his lips and blows. He can make the sounds higher and higher by pushing down one or more of the valves. When he does this, the part of the tube which is sounding is made shorter. You have seen something very like this happen in the stringed instruments. For every time a violinist presses his finger on a string, he shortens it, and the shorter he makes it, the higher he raises his tones. It is polite to sit still at a concert, but when the trumpet blows, you wish you could stand up and cheer. You think of soldiers on parade, or "Hats off! The flag is passing by!" In fact, the trumpet was heard long ago on battlefields where it gave courage and strength to soldiers. At royal celebrations, kings used it because it sounded so grand and important. Helen Keller, who has been blind and deaf since the age of two, was once asked what she imagined the color "red" to be. Her answer was that it seemed like the powerful blast of a trumpet. And this is just what the trumpet's sound is like — a flash of the brightest color we know.

● The trombone is like a trumpet but has a much deeper, sadder and more serious tone. It sounds older and does not jump about so friskily. As you can see, its tube is much longer. There are really two long, thin, U-shaped tubes which slide in and out of one another like a telescope. This is why it is called a slide trombone. The player has usually no valves to push. To play high notes, he slides one tube into the other and shortens it; to get booming low notes, he stretches the tube as far out as his arm can reach. This instrument can be frightening because so much sound pours from it in such slow heavy waves. The tones are so deep and steady that it can also sound very imposing. Some-times, a melody is played by different groups of instruments until it get louder and louder and all the air around seems filled with it. When the sound is loudest and most impressive, then you know that the trombones have taken the lead.

● In a sextet, there are six players. In addition to the string quartet there may
be a flute and a French horn.

● Though it is a brass instrument played like the trumpet, the French horn is usually not loud or harsh. It is a happy instrument with a soft and sweet tone which floats through the air clearly and gracefully. Sometimes it sounds shadowy or far away. Its tone is peaceful and quiet, reminding you of hot still days in the shade or of lovely cloudless moonlit nights. So gentle is its voice that composers like to make it play with the woodwinds. In fact, when you first hear it, you may think it is one of them. A special effect is produced when the player puts his right hand into the bell, or large end of the horn. This acts like a mute, and the sound becomes muffled, soft and distant; and the music speaks of magic and mystery. This is an instrument which gives even the best of players a very hard time. Its tones can suddenly begin to wobble, and what comes out is anything but the right note. It is like the little girl in the poem who could be very very good, "but when she was bad, she was horrid." The player cannot help himself when this happens. But everyone knows that you cannot trust a French horn to behave, so he is quickly forgiven.

24

● When we come to the bass tuba, we have reached the last of the brasses. It is quite tremendous. Its tube is longer than the trombone's or French horn's, and it gets wider and wider until its throat and mouth are very large indeed. We know by now that as the body of an instrument gets longer and as the mouth widens, the tone gets lower. The tuba's voice is low and loud, and, because it is such a fat instrument, it gets out of breath quickly. It gasps out deep gruff windy tones sounding like um-pah-pah. It huffs and puffs. It cannot really sing, although, like a drum, it can give "snap" to a dancing rhythm. Usually this giant of the brasses has the same duties as the double bass, the largest of the strings. Its low voice is needed to provide background and weight so that the high tones of the other brasses do not sound top-heavy and unsteady.

● The kettle drum belongs to the large family of percussion instruments. These are struck, some gently and some with a bang, in order to create a special sound effect or to beat time strongly. Because they are so noisy, they are usually placed in the rear of the orchestra. The kettle drum stands out among the drums because it alone can be tuned to different levels of pitch. The others produce sounds that are unchanging except that they may be louder or softer. There are usually two kettle drums with rounded bottoms. The largest one naturally has the lowest sound. To change the tone, the drummer tightens or loosens screws on the sides. He uses both hands for playing, and sometimes you see them move with great speed as he produces a "roll" like thunder. If he beats hard, the thunder seems near and frightening. If he beats lightly, the thunder seems far away and strange. For a loud thud, he uses a stick with a leather head; for a duller noise, he uses one that is covered with lamb's wool.

● The snare drum was once carried to the wars on the hip of the drummer boy. It went right along with the soldiers into battle. It is much smaller than the kettle drum. It is played with two wooden sticks. The skins stretched over the top and bottom are called "heads." This drum gets its name from the snares — thin strings — stretched across the lower head. When the player beats the upper head, these snares rattle against the lower one. The snare drum is a military drum with a sharper and snappier sound than the kettle drum. It beats out march rhythms in a rat-a-tat-tat, rat-a-tat-tat. It makes you think of battles, parades and soldiers marching in formation.

● The bass drum is the largest and heaviest of the drums, about four times as large as the snare drum. It has a wooden frame with two parchment heads. It is placed on its side and played with only one stick, the end of which is covered with leather or lamb's wool depending on whether one wants it to sound more or less booming. It raises thunderous echoes with each beat. When the beats follow one another quickly, the echoes clash and the air seems heavy with threatening sound. The bass drum can also sound very solemn. When it beats time slowly and steadily, it can make you feel as if it were warning of danger or despair. It almost says, "Beware! Beware!"

● The triangle is simply a steel rod bent into a three-cornered shape with its two ends close together but not touching. When it is tapped with a little steel rod, it gives out a bell-like sound. But it must be held in the air hanging from a cord and not allowed to touch any other surface, or you will hear not a tinkle but a dull knock. Try hitting two horseshoes against one another and see for yourself that this is so.

● The gong is an old Chinese instrument. Like the triangle, it must be held in the air in order to vibrate freely. It is a large round brass plate with its edge rounded back. Its surface is uneven. When it is struck with a bass drum stick, you hear a "bong" that sounds very close and then a crash which fades away.

29

● The castanets are strange little noise-makers. Because they are made of wood, they click instead of booming like the hollow drum or crashing like the metal gong. They are two little wooden clappers with a space hollowed out in the middle of the sides that face one another. They give zip to a dance tune.

● The tambourine is a drum with only one head and with many little metal discs which jingle all around it. The player either shakes it while holding it in his left hand or strikes it with his right hand. It sounds something like this: jingle, thump, thump, jingle, thump, knock, jingle, jingle, jingle, thump. It is a merry instrument and makes you think of people dancing and laughing.

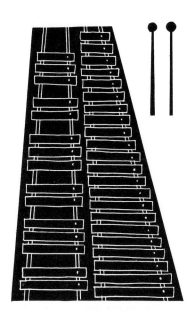

● The xylophone, unlike most percussion instruments, can play a tune. Because of this, it belongs to a separate branch of the percussion family which includes the chimes, the celesta and the glockenspiel. It lies flat before the player with its two rows of wooden slats arranged like the black and white keys of the piano. It is played with two light hammers which strike the slats much as fingers strike the keys on a piano. Each tone is a short "clink." When the whole orchestra wants to make you smile or laugh, it calls on the xylophone to perform its tricks. Its odd unexpected sound always has a comic effect.

● The crash in the orchestra when the music has been especially loud and exciting is most probably the sound of the cymbals. These are two metal plates which the player strikes one against the other in a side-swiping motion. Sometimes one of the plates is struck sharply with a drumstick; then the crash is not so loud. A deafening effect can be got by using two drumsticks on one cymbal. The player keeps striking the cymbal very quickly, first with one stick and then with the other. He begins softly and gradually plays louder and louder until there is no more loudness left. No one would want to use the cymbals or the big bass drum so often that the noise got tiresome and annoying. Sometimes one of the cymbals with its face up is attached to the bass drum so that both instruments can be played by one performer.

● The sound of church bells is produced in the orchestra by the chimes. This instrument is made up of a row of metal pipes hung from a frame. They are struck with a small wooden mallet. As the player looks from left to right, the pipes get shorter and the tones you hear get higher. The chimes sound much more like real bells than do the celesta or the glockenspiel. When you hear chimes, the music is serious, solemn and religious. You feel as if you were in a large cathedral with the congregation deep in prayer. The chimes can play only a slow simple melody or single tones that are far apart. They do not sound well when played fast because the sound of each tone lingers for a long while before it dies out. If many tones are struck quickly one after another, you hear a very unpleasant jumble of sound.

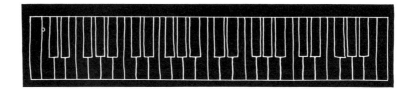

● The celesta looks like a little upright piano and is played like one. True to its name — which means "heavenly," — its sound is sweet and clear like that of delightful silver and golden bells. It can make you think of light and graceful spirits dancing in the air. Like the chimes the celesta can play a melody, but unlike them it can play it fast. In fact the celesta sounds better when played rapidly. It has one weakness: it can be drowned out very easily. When the celesta plays, the music must be soft and hushed.

● The glockenspiel looks very much like a xylophone and is played in the same way. Its slats are made of metal instead of wood, however. They are struck with two little wooden hammers. The sounds are like those of little bells, bright and metallic. The glockenspiel often plays the melody together with one or more of the woodwind instruments like the piccolo, flute, clarinet or oboe. Then it seems to add a bright edge to the melody.

● At one time or another, many additional percussion instruments have been used in the orchestra — such as cowbells, wind machines and rattles. They are too many to mention. In fact, almost any object that can make a sound has found its way into the percussion section. That is why this part of the orchestra is often referred to as the "kitchen."

● The conductor also plays an instrument. His instrument is the whole orchestra. He knows all the parts. It is his job to make the instruments sound well together and to train the players to say most beautifully what the composer had in his heart. A conductor must be an expert in three different fields. He must be a

leader whom the players respect, trust and follow. He must also be a good teacher, patient and able to explain so that the players will understand exactly what is wanted. Lastly, he must be an interpreter; that is, through his own understanding of the music, he must help the listener appreciate what the music has to say.

INDEX